A Note to Parents and Teachers

DK READERS is a compelling program for beginning readers, designed in conjunction with literacy experts, including Dr. Linda Gambrell, Professor of Education at Clemson University. Dr. Gambrell served as President of the International Reading Association, National Reading Conference, and College Reading Association.

Beautiful illustrations and superb full-color photographs combine with engaging, easy-to-read stories and informational texts to offer a fresh approach to each subject in the series. Each DK READER is guaranteed to capture a child's interest while developing his or her reading skills, general knowledge, and love of reading.

The five levels of DK READERS are aimed at different reading abilities, enabling you to choose the books that are exactly right for your child:

Pre-level 1: Learning to read

Level 1: Beginning to read

Level 2: Beginning to read alone

Level 3: Reading alone

Level 4: Proficient readers

The "normal" age at which a child begins to read can be anywhere from three to eight years old. Adult participation through the lower levels is very helpful for providing encouragement, discussing storylines, and sounding out unfamiliar words.

No matter which level you select, you can be sure that you are helping your child learn to read, then read to learn!

LONDON, NEW YORK,
MELBOURNE, MUNICH, and DELHI

For Dorling Kindersley
Project Editor Heather Scott
Designer Jason Wilkins
Senior Designer Ron Stobbart
Managing Editor Catherine Saunders
Brand Manager Lisa Lanzarini
Publishing Manager Simon Beecroft
Category Publisher Alex Allan
Production Controller Poppy Newdick
Production Editor Sean Daly

For Lucasfilm
Executive Editor Jonathan W. Rinzler
Art Director Troy Alders
Keeper of the Holocron Leland Chee
Director of Publishing Carol Roeder

Reading Consultant
Linda B. Gambrell, Ph.D

First published in the United States in 2009 by
DK Publishing
375 Hudson Street
New York, New York 10014

11 12 10 9 8 7 6 5 4
DD534—05/09
008

DK Books are available at special discounts when purchased in bulk for sales
promotions, premiums, fund-raising, or educational use. For details, contact:
DK Publishing Special Markets, 375 Hudson Street, New York,
New York 10014, SpecialSales@dk.com

Published in Great Britain by Dorling Kindersley Limited.
A catalog record for this book is available from the Library of Congress

ISBN: 978-0-7566-5198-5 (Hardback)
ISBN: 978-0-7566-5199-2 (Paperback)

Color reproduction by MDP, UK
Printed and bound in the U.S.A. by Lake Book Manufacturing, Inc.

Discover more at
www.dk.com
www.starwars.com

**DK READERS**

BEGINNING
2
TO READ ALONE

STAR WARS

THE CLONE WARS

Jedi In Training

Written by Heather Scott

Ahsoka is training to become a Jedi Knight. Ahsoka has already completed many years of training at the Jedi Temple. Now Ahsoka will receive training from Anakin, a young Jedi Knight.

Anakin's missions are dangerous. Ahsoka is brave and clever, but she still has a lot to learn.

Padawan
Apprentice Jedi Knights are called Padawans. Ahsoka is Anakin's Padawan.

Anakin does not
want a Padawan.
But on her first
mission Ahsoka
saves his life.

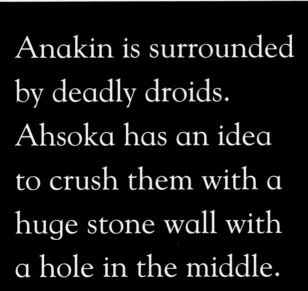

Anakin is surrounded
by deadly droids.
Ahsoka has an idea
to crush them with a
huge stone wall with
a hole in the middle.

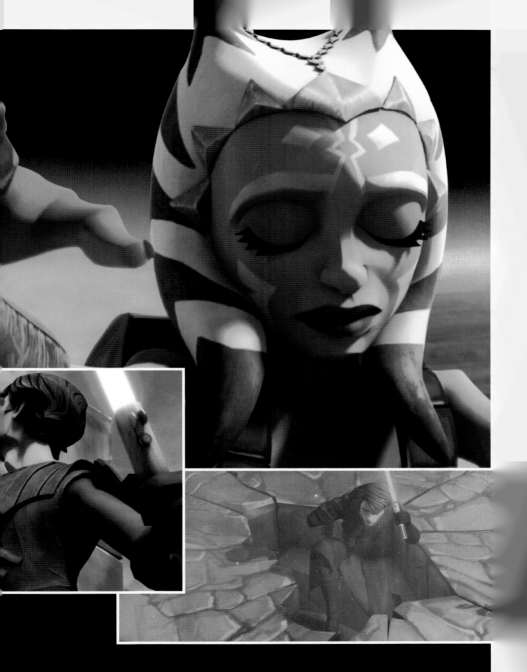

She uses the Force to make the stone wall fall. Anakin is saved!

On their next mission, Anakin and Ahsoka have to rescue Jabba the Hutt's son, Rotta. Rotta was kidnapped and taken to a castle.

When Ahsoka and Anakin find Rotta, he is already sick and needs medicine.

Hutts
Jabba the Hutt is a greedy and powerful criminal. He controls an important part of space that the Jedi would like to fly in.

Someone else has arrived at the
castle. It is Asajj (Ah-SARGE)
Ventress, an enemy of the Jedi.
Ahsoka must escape.

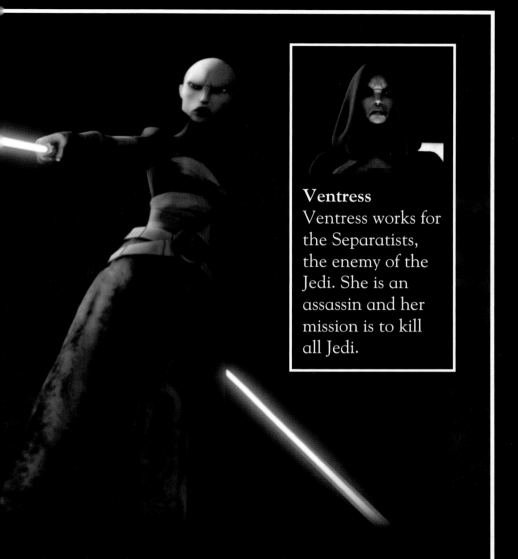

Ventress
Ventress works for the Separatists, the enemy of the Jedi. She is an assassin and her mission is to kill all Jedi.

Ahsoka has to defend herself against Ventress before Anakin comes to rescue her and Rotta on a flying creature.

Ahsoka and Anakin return to
Jabba's planet with Rotta. Ahsoka
has given Rotta some medicine
and he is feeling better.

Jabba is very pleased to see his son
safe and well. He thanks Ahsoka
and Anakin for their help.

Ahsoka and Anakin receive a message that Jedi Plo Koon is in trouble. He has been attacked by the enemy and must defend himself against battle droids.

Plo Koon
Plo Koon is a Jedi Master. He is from the planet Dorin. He is a very brave and clever Jedi.

The Jedi leaders tell
Anakin and Ahsoka
they cannot go to the
rescue. Ahsoka's Jedi instincts tell
her she must go to help him.

Ahsoka and Anakin go to find
Plo Koon and they are just in
time! Ahsoka's Jedi instincts were
right and Plo Koon is still alive.

Ahsoka is very happy to see her old friend. She is glad she trusted her Jedi instincts and disobeyed the Jedi leaders.

Jedi instincts
Jedi feel strongly if something is right or wrong, or safe or not safe. Their feelings are connected to the Force.

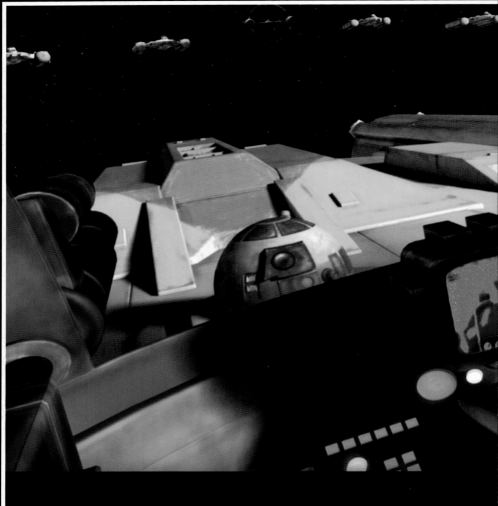

Now Ahsoka and Anakin must destroy the *Malevolence*, the enemy ship that attacked Plo Koon. Anakin has a risky plan to attack the ship's bridge.

Y-Wing
Y-wings are
spaceships that
are fast and
powerful.

Malevolence
The *Malevolence* is
a deadly enemy
ship with a
secret weapon.

Anakin's team of Y-wings fly into
battle but some are shot down.
Ahsoka thinks they need a new
plan. They attack the secret
weapon instead. It is a success!

When Anakin's droid, R2-D2, goes missing after a space battle, Anakin is sent a new droid. Ahsoka welcomes the new droid, who is called R3-S6.

R2-D2
R2-D2 is an astromech droid. He helps Anakin to fly his spaceship and to do any repairs he needs.

Ahsoka tells Anakin that R3 droids are better than R2 droids, but Anakin wants to find R2-D2. They think R2-D2 is on an enemy base, so they go to investigate.

At the enemy base, another Jedi enemy called General Grievous (GREEVE-us) suddenly appears. He attacks Ahsoka, but she hides in the shadows.

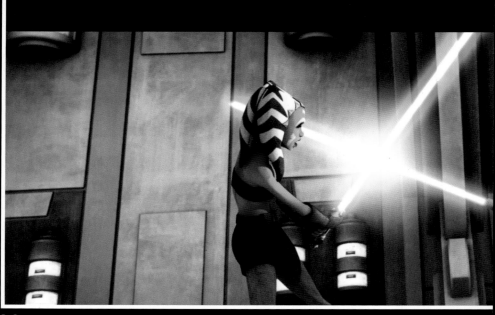

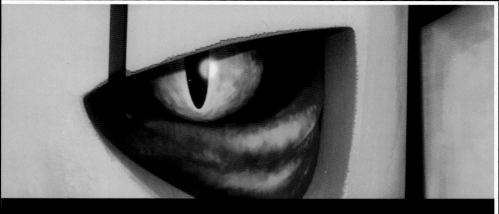

R3-S6 shines a light on Ahsoka.
R3-S6 is a traitor and a spy for
Grievous! Luckily, Ahsoka gets
away. Anakin finds R2-D2 and
they all escape the enemy base.

Ahsoka goes on a mission with
Jedi Master Luminara. They are
taking a prisoner to stand trial.
The prisoner's name is Nute
Gunray. He knows a lot of enemy
secrets, which the
Jedi want to learn.

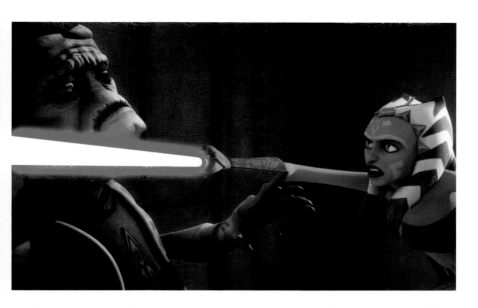

Ahsoka threatens Nute so he will tell them the secrets. Luminara doesn't like Ahsoka threatening Nute and tells her to stop. Ahsoka doesn't like being told what to do.

Ventress and the droid army attack the Jedi ship.

Ventress has come to rescue Nute Gunray. While Luminara is fighting the droids in another part of the ship, Ventress sets Nute Gunray free.

Ventress kicks Ahsoka into Gunray's cell. Gunray gloats as Ahsoka is now a prisoner and not him. Luminara's Jedi instincts tell her that Ahsoka is in danger and she races back to the cell block.

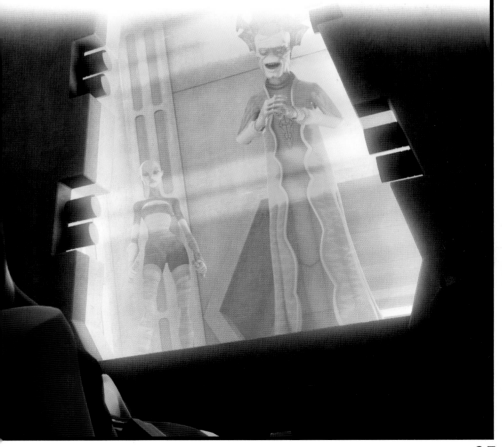

Ventress flees without Nute as
Luminara returns. Luminara lets
Ahsoka out of her cell and puts
Nute back in prison. She tells
Ahsoka to stay and guard Nute
while she deals with Ventress alone.

Ahsoka wants to help Luminara, so she leaves her post. She arrives just in time to save Luminara! They attack Ventress together, but she escapes with Nute! Luminara thanks Ahsoka for saving her life.

Ahsoka has learned a lot.
She has learned to trust her
Jedi instincts. She has learned that
the Jedi's enemies are dangerous
and that they cannot be
fought alone.

She has learned to work as a team with the other Jedi. Most of all, she has learned that she has what it takes to become a great Jedi Knight!

Throughout her adventures, Ahsoka has made some friends and enemies.

Ahsoka's friends:

Anakin

Luminara

Plo Koon

R2-D2

Ahsoka's enemies:

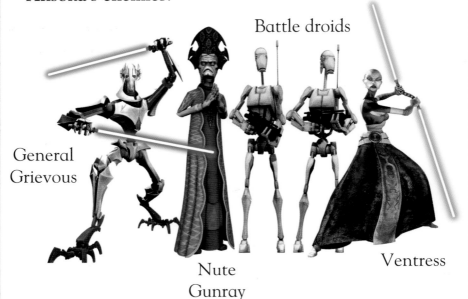

Battle droids

General Grievous

Nute Gunray

Ventress